The Collegeville Prayer of the Faithful Annual, 2007
Cycle C

Michael Kwatera, O.S.B.

LITURGICAL PRESS
Collegeville, Minnesota

www.litpress.org

Cover design by Monica Bokinskie.

© 2006 by Order of Saint Benedict, Collegeville, Minnesota. All rights reserved. No part of this book may be reproduced in any form, by print, microfilm, microfiche, mechanical recording, photocopying, translation, or by any other means, known or yet unknown, for any purpose except brief quotations in reviews, without the previous written permission of Liturgical Press, Saint John's Abbey, P.O. Box 7500, Collegeville, Minnesota 56321-7500. Printed in the United States of America.

ISSN 1931-4124

ISBN 13: 978-0-8146-3051-8
ISBN 10: 0-8146-3051-0

In memory of
Teri Luann Dlugosch
1951–2006
musician, liturgist, friend

Contents

Liturgical Year C

Introduction   8
First Sunday of Advent   *December 3, 2006*   12
Immaculate Conception   *December 8, 2006*   14
Second Sunday of Advent   *December 10, 2006*   16
Our Lady of Guadalupe   *December 12, 2006*   18
Third Sunday of Advent   *December 17, 2006*   20
Fourth Sunday of Advent   *December 24, 2006*   22
Christmas Eve   *December 24, 2006*   24
Christmas Day   *December 25, 2006*   26
Holy Family   *December 31, 2006*   28
Mary, Mother of God   *January 1, 2007*   30
Second Sunday After Christmas   *January 7, 2007*   32
Epiphany of the Lord   *January 7, 2007*   34
Baptism of the Lord   *January 8, 2007*   36
Second Sunday in Ordinary Time   *January 14, 2007*   38
Dr. Martin Luther King Jr. Holiday, U.S.A.   *January 15, 2007*   40
Third Sunday in Ordinary Time   *January 21, 2007*   42
Fourth Sunday in Ordinary Time   *January 28, 2007*   44
Fifth Sunday in Ordinary Time   *February 4, 2007*   46
Sixth Sunday in Ordinary Time   *February 11, 2007*   48

Contents

Seventh Sunday in Ordinary Time *February 18, 2007* 50
Ash Wednesday *February 21, 2007* 52
First Sunday of Lent *February 25, 2007* 54
Second Sunday of Lent *March 4, 2007* 56
Third Sunday of Lent *March 11, 2007* 58
Fourth Sunday of Lent *March 18, 2007* 60
St. Joseph, Husband of the Blessed Virgin Mary *March 19, 2007* 62
Fifth Sunday of Lent *March 25, 2007* 64
Annunciation of the Lord *March 26, 2007* 66
Palm Sunday of the Lord's Passion *April 1, 2007* 68
Holy Thursday *April 5, 2007* 70
Holy Saturday: Easter Vigil *April 7, 2007* 72
Easter Sunday: The Resurrection of the Lord *April 8, 2007* 74
Second Sunday of Easter *April 15, 2007* 76
Third Sunday of Easter *April 22, 2007* 78
Fourth Sunday of Easter *April 29, 2007* 80
Fifth Sunday of Easter *May 6, 2007* 82
Sixth Sunday of Easter *May 13, 2007* 84
Ascension of the Lord *May 17, 2007* 86
Seventh Sunday of Easter *May 20, 2007* 88
Pentecost *May 27, 2007* 90
Memorial Day, U.S.A. *May 28, 2007* 92
Holy Trinity *June 3, 2007* 94
Body and Blood of Christ *June 10, 2007* 96
Sacred Heart *June 15, 2007* 98
Eleventh Sunday in Ordinary Time *June 17, 2007* 100
Nativity of St. John the Baptist *June 24, 2007* 102
SS. Peter and Paul, Apostles *June 29, 2007* 104
Thirteenth Sunday in Ordinary Time *July 1, 2007* 106
Independence Day, U.S.A. *July 4, 2007* 108
Fourteenth Sunday in Ordinary Time *July 8, 2007* 110
Fifteenth Sunday in Ordinary Time *July 15, 2007* 112

Contents

Sixteenth Sunday in Ordinary Time   *July 22, 2007*   114
Seventeenth Sunday in Ordinary Time   *July 29, 2007*   116
Eighteenth Sunday in Ordinary Time   *August 5, 2007*   118
Nineteenth Sunday in Ordinary Time   *August 12, 2007*   120
Assumption of Mary   *August 15, 2007*   122
Twentieth Sunday in Ordinary Time   *August 19, 2007*   124
Twenty-First Sunday in Ordinary Time   *August 26, 2007*   126
Twenty-Second Sunday in Ordinary Time   *September 2, 2007*   128
Labor Day, U.S.A. and Canada   *September 3, 2007*   130
Twenty-Third Sunday in Ordinary Time   *September 9, 2007*   132
Twenty-Fourth Sunday in Ordinary Time   *September 16, 2007*   134
Twenty-Fifth Sunday in Ordinary Time   *September 23, 2007*   136
Twenty-Sixth Sunday in Ordinary Time   *September 30, 2007*   138
Twenty-Seventh Sunday in Ordinary Time   *October 7, 2007*   140
Twenty-Eighth Sunday in Ordinary Time   *October 14, 2007*   142
Twenty-Ninth Sunday in Ordinary Time   *October 21, 2007*   144
Thirtieth Sunday in Ordinary Time   *October 28, 2007*   146
All Saints   *November 1, 2007*   148
Commemoration of All the Faithful Departed (All Souls)
    November 2, 2007   150
Thirty-First Sunday in Ordinary Time   *November 4, 2007*   152
Thirty-Second Sunday in Ordinary Time   *November 11, 2007*   154
Thirty-Third Sunday in Ordinary Time   *November 18, 2007*   156
Thanksgiving Day, U.S.A., *November 22, 2007*   158
Christ the King   *November 25, 2007*   160

Introduction

When Pope Urban IV asked Thomas Aquinas to compose the Divine Office and Mass texts for the newly-established feast of Corpus Christi (1264), the Dominican friar and theologian professed his unworthiness for so sacred a task. But he completed it beautifully. I am no Thomas Aquinas, yet I, too, feel humbled in preparing this collection of intercessory prayers for the eucharistic liturgy. To place prayerful words on human lips and in human hearts is a most sacred work.

My *Preparing the General Intercessions* (Liturgical Press, 1996) is a practical, "how-to" book for composing the prayer of the faithful for the Eucharist. This present volume is a collection of *almost* ready-to-pray intercessions for the Sundays, solemnities, and some civil holidays of the Lectionary's Year C. I say "almost" because every liturgist and/or pastor will want to include particular persons and needs in the texts found here. Also, matters of immediate concern (for example, local tragedies and natural disasters) will need to be included in these rather general texts. Often the intentions can be made more "local" by changing the persons to be prayed for. To facilitate this, a disk containing Microsoft Word files of these texts according to calendar date has been included at the back of this volume.

Preparing prayers for the Christian assembly to pray is a challenging but rewarding task. It took some courage for the Catholic Church to permit clergy and laypersons to prepare the prayer of the faithful for their congregations rather than legislating mandatory texts for use by the entire church. Thus, the General Instruction of the Roman Missal (2002) states:

> It is for the priest celebrant to direct this prayer from the chair. He himself begins it with a brief introduction by which he invites the

Introduction

faithful to pray, and likewise he concludes it with a prayer. The intentions announced should be sober, be composed freely but prudently, and be succinct, and they should express the prayer of the entire community (no. 71).

This statement gives generous freedom to those who prepare the prayer of the faithful but also requires careful discipline and theological accuracy in composing this prayer. I hope that such qualities are reflected in the prayer texts offered here.

Annie Dillard wrote about her Congregationalist pastor:

> Once, in the middle of the long pastoral prayer of intercession for the whole world—for the gift of wisdom to its leaders, for hope and mercy to the grieving and pained, succor to the oppressed, and God's grace to all—in the middle of this he stopped, and burst out, "Lord, we bring you these same petitions every week." After a shocked pause, he continued reading the prayer. Because of this, I like him very much.[1]

The Church must pray for the same things every week, because the same human needs are old and new every Sunday in different persons. But these needs can be presented to God in fresh language shaped by the liturgical feasts, seasons and the Sunday Scripture readings, as I have tried to do in this collection. Robert W. Hovda puts it very well: "The general intercessions are not there to impress the world with our knowledge of what is best for everybody. They are there to help worshipers rely more heavily on God's word and on God's Spirit than our own devices—or on the mass media."[2]

In preparing the intentions, I have searched the day's Scripture readings, and especially the responsorial psalm, for a word or phrase that leaps out from the text. Such a word or phrase has often been used in each of the intentions, repeated again and again as the series unfolds. This serves to link the prayer of the faithful to the prayer of the psalm. In this way, a pattern is developed that draws the worshipers into the intentions and provides a certain rhythmic, lyrical quality to them.

---

[1] Annie Dillard, *Holy the Firm* (New York: Harper & Row, 1977) 58–59.
[2] Robert W. Hovda, "Real and Worshipful Intercessions," *Worship* 60:6 (November 1986) 533.

Introduction

As an example of this method, let us turn to the intentions for the Third Sunday of Advent (Year C) included here:

Minister: **For leaders of Christian churches and communities,
that the Lord's strength
will renew them in their responsibilities,
let us pray to the Lord:**

                     **For leaders of governments,
that the Lord's courage
will lead them along the ways of justice and peace,
let us pray to the Lord:**

                     **For the sick and injured,
that the Lord's peace
will stand guard over their lives,
let us pray to the Lord:**

                     **For babies about to be born,
that the Lord's care
will bring them to the fullness of their humanity,
let us pray to the Lord:**

                     **For this assembly of God's people,
that the Lord's presence
will make us a source of spiritual joy for each other,
let us pray to the Lord:**

                     **For those who have died,
especially _____ and _____,
that the Lord's salvation
will fill them with everlasting joy,
let us pray to the Lord:**

These intentions follow the order given in the General Instruction of the Roman Missal (2002):

       a. For the needs of the Church;
       b. For public authorities and the salvation of the whole world;
       c. For those burdened by any kind of difficulty;
       d. For the local community (no. 70).

Introduction

The pattern in these intentions is: For *someone*, that the Lord's *something* will *do something (something good!)* for them, let us pray to the Lord. Additions to this set of intercessions should follow this pattern for the sake of consistency. The pattern in each set of intentions should be easily discernible. This will be helpful as particular intentions are needed, for example, praying for First Communicants and Confirmation candidates, as well as for inviting the assembly to include their personal needs and intentions, if desired. Many of the sets of intentions in this book conclude with such an invitation. Presenting these additions in sense-lines, as has been done in this book, will help lectors to proclaim these texts in the assembly.

Pope Benedict XVI has identified the intercessions as one of the liturgical "opportunities calling for the application of creativity."[3] Thus, the contribution of persons who have the gift of formulating intercessions should be encouraged. This task is properly the work of one gifted person for each occasion. "May he or she be a poet first," says Robert Hovda. "Any other qualifications are secondary."[4] Yes, a poet, because the Greek word "poet" means "creator." Preparing the prayer of the faithful is a craft in the service of the liturgy that requires divine assistance, human skill and the fruitful creativity in which both work together.

Michael Kwatera, O.S.B.
June 29, 2006
Solemnity of SS. Peter and Paul, apostles

---

[3] Cardinal Joseph Ratzinger, "Structure of the Liturgical Celebration," in *The Feast of Faith: Approaches to a Theology of the Liturgy,* trans. Graham Harrison (San Francisco: Ignatius Press, 1986) 68.

[4] Robert W. Hovda, "The Prayer of General Intercession," *Worship* 44:8 (October 1970) 502.

December 3, 2006

FIRST SUNDAY OF ADVENT

Priest: As we begin the season of Advent, let us call upon God our Savior in fervent prayer.

Minister: That the Lord's guidance will be with the leaders of the church, let us pray to the Lord:

That the Lord's justice will be with the leaders of nations, let us pray to the Lord:

That the Lord's kindness will be with those who suffer from hunger and disease, let us pray to the Lord:

That the Lord's constancy will be with all who seek to do God's will, let us pray to the Lord:

That the Lord's friendship will be with all who have died, especially _____ and _____, let us pray to the Lord:

✢

✢

Priest: **Lord God,**
let our prayers at this Eucharist
help us welcome your Son here in our midst
and at the end of time.
We ask this through Christ our Lord. Amen.

December 8, 2006

IMMACULATE CONCEPTION

Priest: In company with the sinless Mother of God,
patroness of the United States,
let us ask God to look upon us with favor,
and to hear the prayers we offer
    for the entire human family.

Minister: For the ministers of the church,
that they preach the message of salvation with
    Mary's humility,
let us pray to the Lord:

    For civil leaders and the citizens of all nations,
that they establish peace and justice with
    Mary's integrity,
let us pray to the Lord:

    For all who suffer from illness or hardship,
that they trust in the surpassing love of God
    with Mary's perseverance,
let us pray to the Lord:

    For parents and their children,
that they serve each other's needs with
    Mary's generosity,
let us pray to the Lord:

    For this assembly,
that we praise God's glory with
    Mary's reverence,
let us pray to the Lord:

**For those who have died,
especially _____ and _____,
that they celebrate around God's throne with
   Mary's joy,
let us pray to the Lord:**

+

+

Priest: **Praise to you, God and Father of our Lord
   Jesus Christ,
for hearing our prayers in your great mercy,
and for bestowing on us
every spiritual blessing for our salvation.
Grant that we, like Mary,
will share abundantly in the holiness of
   your Son,
and praise the divine grace you have given us
   in him,
for ever and ever. Amen.**

December 10, 2006

SECOND SUNDAY OF ADVENT

Priest: The Lord Jesus is always near to us,
always coming into our hearts.
As we await the revelation of Christ's glory at
    the end of the ages,
let us ask God to hear and answer
    these petitions.

Minister: That the Lord will give wisdom
to those who promote the Gospel of Christ,
let us pray to the Lord:

That the Lord will give comfort
to those who live in mourning and misery,
let us pray to the Lord:

That the Lord will give healing
to those who are weakened by sin
    and sickness,
let us pray to the Lord:

That the Lord will give renewed strength
to us who are gathered here,
let us pray to the Lord:

That the Lord will give everlasting glory
to those who have died,
especially _____ and _____,
let us pray to the Lord:

+

+

Priest: Ruler of all times and seasons,
we ask you to fill these days of waiting with
 your saving love.
Deepen our love for you and for each other.
Bring us to glory with your Son, Jesus Christ,
who lives and reigns with you and the
 Holy Spirit,
one God, for ever and ever. Amen.

December 12, 2006

OUR LADY OF GUADALUPE

Priest: The God of glory honored the Blessed
 Virgin Mary
by changing Tepeyac's barren ground
into a fragrant garden of flowers.
Let us ask God
to transform the rough places of our hearts
 and of our world,
so that our lives may bear the imprint of
 Mary's virtues.

Minister: That the all-holy God be the holiness
of those called to share the life of God's Son,
the Savior of all nations,
let us pray to the Lord:

That the all-powerful God be the power
of all who serve in the ordained ministry and
 in the religious life,
let us pray to the Lord:

That the all-saving God be the salvation
of those oppressed by poverty and injustice
 throughout the earth,
let us pray to the Lord:

That the all-protecting God be the protection
 of the Americas
through the intercession of Our Lady of
 Guadalupe, our patroness,
let us pray to the Lord:

That the all-merciful God be the mercy of
 those who have died,
especially _____ and _____,
let us pray to the Lord:

+

+

Priest: Almighty and everlasting God,
you willed that your Word should take flesh
in the womb of the Blessed Virgin Mary.
Grant that we who honor her as Our Lady
 of Guadalupe
may be delivered by her prayers
from all sin and sorrow,
and may be welcomed to the joys of our
 heavenly home.
We ask this through Christ our Lord. Amen.

December 17, 2006

THIRD SUNDAY OF ADVENT

Priest: My brothers and sisters,
let us confidently present our needs to God
and ask God's promised salvation in
these prayers.

Minister: For leaders of Christian churches
and communities,
that the Lord's strength
will renew them in their responsibilities,
let us pray to the Lord:

For leaders of governments,
that the Lord's courage
will lead them along the ways of justice
and peace,
let us pray to the Lord:

For the sick and injured,
that the Lord's peace
will stand guard over their lives,
let us pray to the Lord:

For babies about to be born,
that the Lord's care
will bring them to the fullness of
their humanity,
let us pray to the Lord:

For this assembly of God's people,
that the Lord's presence
will make us a source of spiritual joy for
each other,
let us pray to the Lord:

For those who have died,
especially _____ and _____,
that the Lord's salvation
will fill them with everlasting joy,
let us pray to the Lord:

+

+

Priest: God our Savior, let us draw water joyfully
from the springs of your mercy.
Let us see your greatness in answer to
    our prayers,
for we make them in the name of your Son,
    Jesus Christ,
who is Lord for ever and ever. Amen.

December 24, 2006

FOURTH SUNDAY OF ADVENT

Priest: Our help in every need is from the Lord.
In company with Christ,
let us pray to the God who upholds our lives.

Minister: That the Lord will give new life to the church
as it prepares for the return of its Lord,
let us pray to the Lord:

That the Lord will give new life
to rulers of nations and their people,
let us pray to the Lord:

That the Lord will give new life
to victims of injustice and persecution,
let us pray to the Lord:

That the Lord will give new life
to those who are crushed by poverty
 and illness,
let us pray to the Lord:

That the Lord will give new life
to those who have died,
especially _____ and _____,
let us pray to the Lord:

Let us remember our personal needs.

[pause for silent prayer]

That the Lord will give us new life
in every need,
let us pray to the Lord:

✢

✢

Priest: **Rouse your power, Lord,
in answer to our prayers.
As we turn away from trust in ourselves,
help us turn to trust in you,
the source of new life.
We ask this through Christ our Lord. Amen.**

December 24, 2006

CHRISTMAS EVE

Priest: God so loved the world
that God gave us the only-begotten Son;
in him we become heirs of eternal life as
    God's children.
As we joyfully celebrate God's salvation
made incarnate in Jesus Christ,
let us pray for its fulfillment in ourselves and
    in all people,
even to the ends of the earth.

Minister: That those who lead the church
will behold the salvation of our God
in their ministry of God's grace and mercy,
let us pray to the Lord:

That those who lead nations
will behold the salvation of our God
in their successful efforts for justice
    and peace,
let us pray to the Lord:

That those who suffer from sickness,
    unemployment, and poverty
will behold the salvation of our God
in words of hope and deeds of love,
let us pray to the Lord:

That those who are gathered here
will behold the salvation of our God
in their zeal for all that is right and just,
let us pray to the Lord:

That those who have died,
especially _____ and _____,
will behold the salvation of our God
in the Lord's kindness and faithfulness,
let us pray to the Lord:

+

+

Priest: **Lord, our mighty God,
our gladness on this holy night is
     great indeed,
for we find our everlasting light
in your Son who dwells with us.
In his name, we ask you to hear our prayers
and sustain us in your justice and constancy.
To you, Father, be all glory in the highest,
through Jesus Christ, our Savior,
in the power of the Holy Spirit,
both now and for ever. Amen.**

December 25, 2006

CHRISTMAS DAY

Priest: Christ is born!
The reign of God dawns in our midst.
Let us ask that God's kindness and generous
 love in the Word made flesh
will fill the earth in answer to these prayers.

Minister: For the faithfulness of God
to make the church a holy people,
let us pray to the Lord:

For the peace of God
to gladden all nations on earth,
let us pray to the Lord:

For the comfort of God
to save those afflicted by any need,
especially _____ and _____,
let us pray to the Lord:

For the grace of God
to renew us and all believers in hope,
let us pray to the Lord:

For the glory of God
to fill those who have died,
especially _____ and _____,
let us pray to the Lord:

✙

✙

Priest: **Lord God,**
on this holy day we joyfully proclaim:
in every darkness, Christ our light!
in every weakness, Christ our might!
Let our prayers bring us your favor in him,
both now and for ever. Amen.

December 31, 2006

HOLY FAMILY

Priest: As God's chosen ones,
made holy and beloved through Jesus Christ,
let us ask our Father to receive these prayers
for the human family

Minister: That the leaders of the church
will clothe themselves with Christ
by putting on his self-denial,
let us pray to the Lord:

That the leaders of nations
will clothe themselves with Christ
by putting on his humility,
let us pray to the Lord:

That families will clothe themselves
    with Christ
by putting on his kindness,
let us pray to the Lord:

That the suffering will clothe themselves
    with Christ
by putting on his patience,
let us pray to the Lord:

That we will clothe ourselves with Christ
by putting on his discipleship,
let us pray to the Lord:

That the dead, especially _____ and
_____,
will clothe themselves with Christ
by putting on the glory of his resurrection,
let us pray to the Lord:

+

+

Priest: **God of peace,
you have made us one family in Christ Jesus.
In his name,
we ask you to share with us and with all
 your people
the blessings of your incarnate Son.
Let your everlasting love
bind us close to him and to each other,
this day and every day,
both now and for ever. Amen.**

January 1, 2007

MARY, MOTHER OF GOD

Priest: Now let us ask God's blessing upon the new year through Jesus Christ,
who has become one of us
in all things but sin.

Minister: Christ became like us in our weakness;
may the church become like him in his saving power.
For this, let us pray to the Lord:

Christ became like the poor and the oppressed in their suffering;
may they become like him in his triumph over injustice.
For this, let us pray to the Lord:

Christ became like us in our human lowliness;
may we become like him in his divine glory.
For this, let us pray to the Lord:

Christ became like the dead in their emptiness;
may those who have died,
especially _____ and _____,
become like him in his fullness of life.
For this, let us pray to the Lord:

Christ became like us in our need;
let us now remember our particular needs
on this day of beginnings.

[pause for silent prayer]

For these, let us pray to the Lord:

✙

✙

Priest: **Lord God, with Mary, the Queen of Peace,
we treasure the fulfillment of your promises
    in our lives.
Help us to live as your sons and daughters
in the new year that you give us,
so that with the shepherds
we may praise and glorify you
for your kindness to us in your Son,
    Jesus Christ,
who is Lord for ever and ever. Amen.**

January 7, 2007

SECOND SUNDAY AFTER CHRISTMAS
(where Epiphany is observed on January 6)

Priest: **The Word of God, who was made flesh in Jesus Christ,
is the source of grace and truth for us and for all people.
Let us pray that God's gifts in Christ
will change darkness into light for all the world.**

Minister: **That God's wisdom may dwell in those
who serve the community of believers,
let us pray to the Lord:**

**That God's justice may dwell in those
who are entrusted with public office,
let us pray to the Lord:**

**That God's light may dwell in those
who are overshadowed by suffering and despair,
let us pray to the Lord:**

**That God's favor may dwell in us
who are gathered here,
let us pray to the Lord:**

**That God's glory may dwell in those
who have been called in death to an eternal inheritance,
especially _____ and _____,
let us pray to the Lord:**

✢

✢

Priest: **How wonderful are your works, Lord God!**
In wisdom you have made them all.
Hear us as we pray for every
 spiritual blessing.
Dwell with us, live in us,
as we celebrate the birth of your beloved Son,
 Jesus Christ,
who is Lord for ever and ever. Amen.

January 7, 2007

EPIPHANY OF THE LORD

Priest: Let us raise our eyes to behold the
    Father's glory
shining on the face of Christ,
and devoutly offer these petitions
for ourselves and all humanity.

Minister: That the leaders of the church will
    reveal Christ
through their lives of simplicity and service,
let us pray to the Lord:

That the leaders of governments will
    reveal Christ
through their assistance to exiles and refugees,
let us pray to the Lord:

That those in need of healing,
especially _____ and _____,
    will reveal Christ
through their recovery from sickness,
let us pray to the Lord:

That the members of this assembly will
    reveal Christ
through their renewed dedication to
    his Gospel,
let us pray to the Lord:

That all those who have died,
especially _____ and _____,
    will reveal Christ
through their sharing in his resurrection,
let us pray to the Lord:

        ✢

        ✢

Priest: **God of all peoples,**
we bring before you the gold of your
    divine life,
the incense of our prayer,
and the myrrh of our humanity.
Reveal to us the depths of your love
in the heart of our searching world;
open before us the sea of your riches;
and show us the salvation of your Son,
    Jesus Christ,
who is Lord for ever and ever. Amen.

January 8, 2007

BAPTISM OF THE LORD

Priest: Let us ask God's abundant blessings on us
and on all people through Jesus Christ,
with whom the Father is well pleased.

Minister: For the church,
that we live our baptismal promises as God's
    faithful servants,
let us pray to the Lord:

For government officials,
that they be ministers of justice and peace,
let us pray to the Lord:

For all catechumens,
that they grow in their desire and love
    for Jesus,
let us pray to the Lord:

For those facing decisions about their future,
that they come to know and accept God's will
    for them,
let us pray to the Lord:

For those who have died,
especially _____ and _____,
that they glorify God for ever in heaven,
let us pray to the Lord:

✛

✛

Priest: **Lord God, upholder of all,**
we give you glory in company with Christ,
your beloved Son and chosen Servant.
As you gave your Holy Spirit to him,
so give your Spirit to us.
Renew in us the grace of our baptism,
so that we may serve you as beloved
daughters and sons.
We ask this through Christ our Lord. Amen.

January 14, 2007

SECOND SUNDAY IN ORDINARY TIME

Priest: Let us call on the name of the Lord,
who delights in saving us and caring for us.

Minister: For the holy church of God, its ministers,
and for its renewal throughout the world,
let us pray to the Lord:

For our country, for all nations and peoples,
and for peace in every heart,
let us pray to the Lord:

For the sick, especially _____ and
_____,
for those who care for them,
and for the well-being of all,
let us pray to the Lord:

For married couples, for those preparing
for marriage,
and for all that strengthens mutual love,
let us pray to the Lord:

For those who have died,
especially _____ and _____,
and for the eternal joy of the faithful departed,
let us pray to the Lord:

For those who need our prayers and whom we
now remember:

[pause for silent prayer]

For them and for ourselves,
let us pray to the Lord:

+

+

Priest: Lord God, our needs are great,
but your marvelous deeds for us and for
 all people
are far greater.
Hear and answer the prayers we have made to
 you this day,
for we offer them in the name of your beloved
 Son, Jesus Christ,
who is Lord for ever and ever. Amen.

January 15, 2007

DR. MARTIN LUTHER KING JR. HOLIDAY
(United States of America)

Priest: Blessed be our God
for making peace the fruit of justice and love.
As we honor the memory of Reverend Doctor
  Martin Luther King Jr.,
let us ask God to direct our lives
to bring forth this fruit in harmony.

Minister: That the church will be united and preserved
in the bonds of peace,
let us pray to the Lord:

That civic leaders will promote mutual
  understanding and respect
between different ethnic groups
in our area and throughout the world,
let us pray to the Lord:

That the children of God will enrich
  each other
through their diversity and common goals,
let us pray to the Lord:

That all who suffer from prejudice
  and poverty
will find deliverance in renewed zeal for
  justice throughout our land,
let us pray to the Lord:

That we will rid our hearts of the fear
  and jealousy
that threaten peace in our midst,
let us pray to the Lord:

That those who have died,
especially those martyred in the struggle for
    civil rights,
will live for ever with the God of glory,
let us pray to the Lord:

+

+

Priest: Lord God, creator of the human family,
your Son reconciles us to you and to
    each other.
Answer our prayers in your mercy,
so that the power of Jesus Christ, working
    in us,
will bring all people together in mutual love.
We ask this through the same Christ our Lord.
    Amen.

January 21, 2007

THIRD SUNDAY IN ORDINARY TIME

Priest: **Let us ask to know the Lord's kindness and faithfulness in answer to these prayers.**

Minister: **For the unity of the holy church of God and for the well-being of the human family, let us pray to the Lord:**

For the building of a more humane world and for respect for all human life, let us pray to the Lord:

For the elimination of disease, famine, and war, and for the reconciliation of states and peoples, let us pray to the Lord:

For the recovery of the sick, especially _____ and _____, and for the deliverance of the oppressed, let us pray to the Lord:

For the consolation of the dying, and for the eternal happiness of those who have died, especially _____ and _____, let us pray to the Lord:

✝

✝

Priest: **Lord, let the words of our prayers and the thoughts of our hearts
find favor in your sight,
so that rejoicing in your saving power may be our strength.
We ask this through Christ our Lord. Amen.**

January 28, 2007

FOURTH SUNDAY IN ORDINARY TIME

Priest: Let us call upon our God, who sustains us in good times and bad.

Minister: For the church,
that its ministers and people reveal the reign of God in this world,
let us pray to the Lord:

For all nations, peoples and communities,
that they accept God's call to live in holiness and peace,
let us pray to the Lord:

For the poor and the oppressed,
that their cries for justice be
quickly answered,
let us pray to the Lord:

For ourselves,
that we be strong in faith and generous
in love,
let us pray to the Lord:

For those who have died,
especially _____ and _____,
that they receive the joys of everlasting life,
let us pray to the Lord:

✛

✛

Priest: God of love, our refuge and strength,
we ask you to answer these prayers.
Be for us a helper close at hand in all
 our needs.
We ask this in the name of Jesus the Lord.
 Amen.

February 4, 2007

FIFTH SUNDAY IN ORDINARY TIME

Priest: In the sight of the angels,
let us call upon the name of the Lord
and ask to receive God's everlasting love.

Minister: That God's holiness
will sanctify all servants of the Gospel,
let us pray to the Lord:

That God's truth
will guide public officials in every land,
let us pray to the Lord:

That God's deliverance
will console the hungry and the homeless,
let us pray to the Lord:

That God's healing
will save the sick and the injured,
especially _____ and _____,
let us pray to the Lord:

That God's strength
will empower those with disabilities,
let us pray to the Lord:

That God's kindness
will lead us to give thanks to the Lord in
    this Eucharist,
let us pray to the Lord:

**That God's salvation
will become the praise of those who
 have died,
especially _____ and _____,
let us pray to the Lord:**

+

+

Priest: **Great is your glory, Lord,
in making us followers of your Son,
 Jesus Christ.
Grant us what we need
to complete your work in us and through us.
We ask this through the same Christ our Lord.
 Amen.**

February 11, 2007

SIXTH SUNDAY IN ORDINARY TIME

Priest: Let us place our trust in the Lord,
who is eager to give us what we ask in
these prayers.

Minister: That the church will know God's blessing
in preaching the Gospel of the risen Christ,
let us pray to the Lord:

That the United Nations and
international organizations
will know God's blessing
in their efforts for peace and justice,
let us pray to the Lord:

That, as we observe World Marriage Day,
wives and husbands will know God's blessing
in their mutual love,
let us pray to the Lord:

That the sick will know God's blessing
in restored health and wholeness,
let us pray to the Lord:

That those who lack food, shelter,
and clothing
will know God's blessing in our
abundant generosity,
let us pray to the Lord:

That those who have died,
especially _____ and _____,
will know God's blessing in eternal life,
let us pray to the Lord:

+

+

Priest: **Lord, we ask you to answer these prayers.
As you turn your heart to us in blessing,
turn our hearts to you in hope and love.
We ask this through Christ our Lord. Amen.**

February 18, 2007

SEVENTH SUNDAY IN ORDINARY TIME

Priest: The Lord pardons our iniquities and heals our ills.
Let us ask to become God's pardon and healing for others
in these petitions.

Minister: For divine and human goodness in all believers,
let us pray to the Lord:

For divine and human compassion in all who govern,
let us pray to the Lord:

For divine and human compassion toward victims of famine, disease, and violence,
let us pray to the Lord:

For divine and human mercy in every heart,
let us pray to the Lord:

For divine and human remembrance of those who have died,
especially _____ and _____,
let us pray to the Lord:

✢

✢

Priest: **Lord God, your gifts to us are overflowing.**
Answer our prayers,
so that your abundant generosity to us
will become our gift to others in your name.
We ask this through Christ our Lord. Amen.

February 21, 2007

ASH WEDNESDAY

Priest: Let us present our needs to God,
who is gracious and merciful,
slow to anger and abounding in love.

Minister: For the church,
that it be an ambassador for Christ to
    the world
by announcing the good news
    of reconciliation,
let us pray to the Lord:

For catechumens, soon to become the elect,
that they come to true conversion
as they prepare for baptism at Easter,
let us pray to the Lord:

For those who hold public office,
that they use their authority
to safeguard the well-being and dignity of all,
let us pray to the Lord:

For all who are in agony of mind or body,
that by our friendship and help
God's love be made present to them,
let us pray to the Lord:

For ourselves,
that this Lenten season prepare us
for our passover from death to newness of life,
let us pray to the Lord:

For those who have died,
especially _____ and _____,
that they rejoice for ever in their salvation,
let us pray to the Lord:

+

+

Priest: God ever-faithful,
have mercy on your Church in its need.
As we turn away from sin,
help us turn to you in repentance.
As we leave sinfulness behind,
let us embrace your holiness with all
    our hearts.
We ask this through Christ our Lord. Amen.

February 25, 2007

FIRST SUNDAY OF LENT

Priest: In the spirit of Jesus,
who offered fervent prayer to his Father in
the desert,
let us pray as God's repentant people.

Minister: That Christians everywhere may be
responsive to the Word of God
during this holy season,
let us pray to the Lord:

That government leaders may work for peace
and make these days the acceptable time of
God's salvation,
let us pray to the Lord:

That those who are suffering from physical
illness or emotional distress
may know that God is for them in their need,
let us pray to the Lord:

That we who celebrate this Eucharist
may find strength to walk in God's ways of
love and truth,
let us pray to the Lord:

That all whose journey through this life
    has ended,
especially _____ and _____,
may joyfully enter their eternal home
    in heaven,
let us pray to the Lord:

+

+

Priest: Lord God, defender of the tempted,
help your people turn again to you,
and serve you with all their hearts.
With confidence in your power over evil
we have asked your help;
may we know your mercy and love in
    our lives.
We make this prayer through Christ our Lord.
    Amen.

March 4, 2007

SECOND SUNDAY OF LENT

Priest: Let us present our needs to the Father,
who speaks to us through the beloved Son.

Minister: That the leaders of the church
will listen to the voice of God's Son
in their work for unity among Christians,
let us pray to the Lord:

That world leaders will listen to the voice of
　　God's Son
in their work for peace among nations,
let us pray to the Lord:

That families will listen to the voice of
　　God's Son
in their times of sorrow and their times of joy,
let us pray to the Lord:

That the dead,
especially _____ and _____,
will hear the voice of God's Son inviting them
　　to enter his kingdom,
let us pray to the Lord:

Let us listen to the voice of God's Son
as we remember our personal needs in silence.

　　[pause for silent prayer]

For these intentions, let us pray to the Lord:

✛

✛

Priest: Father, your favor rests on your Son, Jesus, and on those who listen to him.
Give us the wisdom to listen to his words;
give us the strength to share in his sufferings;
give us the grace to share in his resurrection,
both now and for ever. Amen.

March 11, 2007

THIRD SUNDAY OF LENT

Priest: **In company with Christ, the source of our salvation, let us offer our fervent prayers to the God of mercy.**

Minister: **That all Christians will bless the Lord through their generous self-sacrifice, let us pray to the Lord:**

That those who are preparing for baptism and for reception into the Catholic Church will bless the Lord in faith and love, let us pray to the Lord:

That citizens of this and every land will bless the Lord through their pursuit of justice and peace, let us pray to the Lord:

That our parish community will bless the Lord through our Lenten prayer, fasting, and works of charity, let us pray to the Lord:

That those who have died, especially _____ and _____, will bless the Lord for the divine gift of eternal life, let us pray to the Lord:

✝

✝

Priest: **Merciful and gracious God,
we ask you to receive our prayers
and answer them according to your
　　loving-kindness.
Grant that our death and burial with Christ
　　in baptism
may produce an abundant harvest for eternity.
We ask this through Christ our Lord. Amen.**

March 18, 2007

FOURTH SUNDAY OF LENT

Priest: Together let us seek the Lord as we offer
 our petitions
and take refuge in the Lord's abundant mercy.

Minister: That the ministers of the church will taste the
 Lord's goodness
in their service to God's people,
let us pray to the Lord:

That those chosen for Christian initiation
 at Easter
will taste the Lord's goodness
in these final weeks of preparation,
let us pray to the Lord:

That the President, the Congress, and the
 judiciary will taste the Lord's goodness
in their efforts for peace and justice,
let us pray to the Lord:

That the poor will taste the Lord's goodness
in our generous works of charity,
let us pray to the Lord:

That we who worship here will taste the
 Lord's goodness
on our journey to holy Easter,
let us pray to the Lord:

That those who have died,
especially _____ and _____,
will taste the Lord's goodness
in the gift of everlasting joy,
let us pray to the Lord:

+

+

Priest: **Lord God, your Son leads us on the way
of reconciliation.
Let our prayers draw us to him in
this Eucharist,**
so that we may rejoice in him now,
and live with him in your presence,
for ever and ever. Amen.

March 19, 2007

ST. JOSEPH, HUSBAND OF THE BLESSED VIRGIN MARY

Priest: In company with Saint Joseph, head of the Holy Family,
let us ask God's blessing upon the human family in these prayers.

Minister: With Joseph most strong, we ask protection for the holy church of God throughout the world.
For this we pray:

With Joseph most prudent, we ask for right judgment
in all who govern.
For this we pray:

With Joseph most just, we ask justice
for oppressed workers of the earth.
For this we pray:

With Joseph most obedient,
we ask for hearts ready to do God's work.
For this we pray:

With Joseph most faithful, we ask God's mercy upon those who are dying
and upon those who have entered God's rest,
especially _____ and _____.
For this we pray:

✢

✢

Priest: **Merciful God,**
be close to us these Lenten days
as you were close to Saint Joseph, the husband
	of Mary.
Help us to serve you as joyfully as he did,
so that we may join him in the glory
	of heaven,
for ever and ever. Amen.

March 25, 2007

FIFTH SUNDAY OF LENT

Priest: Let us ask God to restore us and all people,
in body, soul, and spirit,
as we make our petitions.

Minister: For God's people throughout the world,
and for those who lack faith and trust in God,
let us pray to the Lord:

For those who exercise authority over others,
and for those who use violence to maintain
their power,
let us pray to the Lord:

For those soon to be initiated and received
into the church,
and for their catechists, sponsors,
and families,
let us pray to the Lord:

For all who are weak and powerless,
especially those addicted to drugs, alcohol,
and gambling,
let us pray to the Lord:

For us assembled here,
and for all who are seeking to know
Christ Jesus
during these Lenten days,
let us pray to the Lord:

For the faithful departed,
especially _____ and _____,
and for all who await resurrection from
 the dead,
let us pray to the Lord:

+

+

Priest: Great are the wonders, Lord,
that you worked for your people Israel in
 ages past.
With them, we ask your eternal and
 merciful love,
today and every day,
both now and for ever. Amen.

March 26, 2007

ANNUNCIATION OF THE LORD

Priest: In the fullness of time, God announced
 to Mary
the great dignity of the only Son.
Her heart became radiant
with the dawning light of our salvation.
Let us ask God to pour forth abundant grace
into our hearts.

Minister: That God will renew the hearts of
 all Christians
with the announcement of enduring love,
let us pray to the Lord:

That God will steady the hearts of
 expectant parents
with the announcement of divine care,
let us pray to the Lord:

That God will refresh the hearts of the poor
with the announcement of speedy deliverance,
let us pray to the Lord:

That God will calm the hearts of those in the
 shadow of death
with the announcement of faithful protection,
let us pray to the Lord:

That God will cheer the hearts of those who
 have died,
especially _____ and _____,
with the announcement of eternal life,
let us pray to the Lord:

+

+

Priest: **Almighty, ever-living God,
your will for humanity is that none should
    be lost
and that all should be saved in Jesus Christ.
Join our prayers to those of the Blessed
    Virgin Mary,
so that your church may do your will joyfully
during this holy season.
We ask this through Christ our Lord. Amen.**

April 1, 2007

PALM SUNDAY OF THE LORD'S PASSION

Priest: My sisters and brothers, as Easter draws near,
let us earnestly pray to the Lord our God.
With deep faith,
let us ask that we who are baptized,
those preparing for Christian initiation, and
 the entire world,
will share more fully in the life of Christ.

Minister: That the church will become more like
 Jesus Christ
in his journey through suffering to glory,
let us pray to the Lord:

That leaders of nations will become like the
 Son of David in his humility,
let us pray to the Lord:

That those whose lives are poured out
 in anguish
will become like the crucified Lord
in his love for others,
let us pray to the Lord:

That we who enter this Holy Week
will become like God's Suffering Servant
in his passover from death to life,
let us pray to the Lord:

That those who have died,
especially _____ and _____,
will become like their risen Savior
in his triumph over death,
let us pray to the Lord:

+

+

Priest: Merciful Father, by the death of Jesus,
　　　your Son,
you showed us the way to everlasting life.
Help us to accept your will for us
as obediently and confidently as he did.
Through these prayers, let us share your life
　　　and love,
for ever and ever. Amen.

April 5, 2007

HOLY THURSDAY

Priest: As we recall the night when Jesus gave us
a living sign of his enduring love,
let us bring our prayers before our
gracious God.

Minister: Christ nourishes the church through
the Eucharist.
By this sacrament, may he root our lives in
his death
and prepare us for his coming in glory.
For this, let us pray to the Lord:

Christ spreads a table where all are nourished.
May we advance along the paths of justice
and peace
in the strength of this food.
For this, let us pray to the Lord:

Christ's sacrifice opens us to life
in all its fullness and mystery.
May we sacrifice ourselves
for all who are starved in spirit, mind, or body.
For this, let us pray to the Lord:

Christ washed the feet of his disciples.
May we learn that the gift of salvation
binds us to serve each other in humility.
For this, let us pray to the Lord:

Christ gives us the Eucharist as the pledge of
    everlasting life.
May those who have died,
especially _____ and _____,
find lasting joy at the banquet in heaven.
For this, let us pray to the Lord:

+

+

Priest: God of love, hear the prayers we offer you
at this commemoration of your Son's life,
    death, and resurrection.
Fill us with his life through our sharing of
    this meal,
and answer our needs in your
    loving-kindness.
We ask this in the name of Jesus, our Lord
    and brother,
through whom we make our thanksgiving
    to you,
both now and for ever. Amen.

April 7, 2007

HOLY SATURDAY: EASTER VIGIL

Priest: With hearts filled with Easter joy,
let us bring our prayers to the God
who raised Jesus from the dead,
confident that the love of the Lord
    is everlasting.

Minister: For the holy church of God throughout
    the world,
especially its newly baptized and
    received members,
that God's people share their Savior's triumph
over sin and death,
let us pray to the Lord:

For the rulers of nations,
that they lead us in turning oppression and
    violence into justice and peace,
let us pray to the Lord:

For those who are discouraged, depressed,
    or despairing,
that they find renewed hope
in the power of Jesus' resurrection,
let us pray to the Lord:

For this community of faith,
dead and risen with Christ,
that we remain grateful for the blessings
    of Lent
and rejoice in the greater blessings of Easter,
let us pray to the Lord:

For those who have died,
especially _____ and _____,
that they celebrate the eternal Easter of life
    and love in God's presence,
let us pray to the Lord:

+

+

Priest: Lord God, your power is beyond compare,
and your love for us is beyond words
    to describe.
In your compassion,
answer the prayers of your ransomed people,
and grant us the riches of your mercy.
We ask this in the name of your risen Son,
    Jesus Christ,
who is Lord for ever and ever. Amen.

April 8, 2007

EASTER SUNDAY: THE RESURRECTION OF THE LORD

Priest: On this festival day,
let us present our petitions to almighty God
through Jesus Christ, our life and
our resurrection.

Minister: That the church will rejoice in
Christ's triumph
over sin and death,
let us pray to the Lord:

That those who are baptized and received into
the church this Easter
will rejoice in peace from on high,
let us pray to the Lord:

That the nations of the world will rejoice in
deliverance from war
and from every threat to human life,
let us pray to the Lord:

That this assembly
will rejoice in the power flowing from
Christ's resurrection,
let us pray to the Lord:

That those who have died,
especially _____ and _____,
will rejoice for ever in glory with their
risen Savior,
let us pray to the Lord:

✢

✢

Priest: **Lord God, you did not forget your beloved
 Son in death,
but raised him to life on the third day.
In his most sacred name,
we ask you to answer our prayers.
Let us share the joy of heaven,
today and every day, both now and for ever.
 Amen.**

April 15, 2007

SECOND SUNDAY OF EASTER
(Divine Mercy Sunday)

Priest: Let us bring our prayers to the Father though Jesus Christ,
the glorious victor over sin and death.

Minister: That the church may be renewed in the joy of its Lord's resurrection,
let us pray to the Lord:

That the nations of the world may receive mercy in the name of Jesus Christ,
let us pray to the Lord:

That those who were baptized into Christ at Easter
may rejoice in peace from on high and the salvation of their souls,
let us pray to the Lord:

That we, like Thomas,
may acclaim Jesus as our Lord and our God,
let us pray to the Lord:

That those who have died,
especially _____ and _____,
may live with their risen Savior for ever,
let us pray to the Lord:

✝

✝

Priest: **God of glory,
you raised our Lord Jesus Christ from
 the dead
and made him the joy of all believers.
Bring us to new life in Christ,
so that we may join those who now see him in
 his risen glory,
and share the blessedness of his kingdom,
both now and for ever. Amen.**

April 22, 2007

THIRD SUNDAY OF EASTER

Priest: In the saving name of Jesus,
let us offer fervent prayer for all in need.

Minister: That the Lord's power will renew the church
in the joy of Christ's resurrection,
let us pray to the Lord:

That the Lord's peace will rescue nations and
peoples from hatred and violence,
let us pray to the Lord:

That the Lord's gifts of living waters and
fertile soil
will sustain the human family,
let us pray to the Lord:

That the Lord's victory over evil will fill our
hearts with thanksgiving and praise,
let us pray to the Lord:

That the Lord's salvation will give
everlasting joy
to those who have died,
especially _____ and _____,
let us pray to the Lord:

    +

    +

Priest: **God, our helper,**
look upon us in your compassion
and grant us the riches of your kindness.
For the blessings we have received
and for those yet to come,
all honor, glory and praise are your due,
    O God,
for ever and ever. Amen.

April 29, 2007

FOURTH SUNDAY OF EASTER

Priest: Let us come before the Lord, our gladness, with these petitions.

Minister: That those who shepherd the holy church of God
will find strength in God's Word,
let us pray to the Lord:

That those who are discerning a church vocation
will find joy in God's call,
let us pray to the Lord:

That those who suffer from sickness and weakness
will find courage in God's faithfulness,
let us pray to the Lord:

That those who lack sufficient food or adequate medical care
will find assistance in God's people,
let us pray to the Lord:

That those who have died,
especially _____ and _____,
will find salvation in God's everlasting life,
let us pray to the Lord:

✚

✚

Priest: **Lord God,
we hunger and thirst for your
  loving-kindness.
Care for us well in answer to these prayers,
so that we may follow your Son to glory
and live with him in your presence,
for ever and ever. Amen.**

May 6, 2007

FIFTH SUNDAY OF EASTER

Priest: Let us pray that the salvation won by
Jesus Christ
will bear fruit in our world
in answer to these prayers.

Minister: For ministers of the church,
that they live in Christ's love
through the strength of God,
let us pray to the Lord:

For those baptized at Easter,
that they live in Christ's love
through the favor of God,
let us pray to the Lord:

For those who lack food, housing,
and employment,
that they live in Christ's love
through the generosity of God at our hands,
let us pray to the Lord:

For those who suffer from illness of mind
or body,
especially children who are abused,
that they live in Christ's love
through the healing of God,
let us pray to the Lord:

For us who worship here,
that we live in Christ's love
through the kindness of God,
let us pray to the Lord:

For those who have died,
especially _____ and _____,
that they live for ever in Christ's love
through the mercy of God,
let us pray to the Lord:

+

+

Priest: God of love,
you have revealed your compassion to us in
 the risen Lord.
Give answer to our prayers,
so that we may love one another
as Christ has loved us,
and praise your name for ever and ever. Amen.

May 13, 2007

SIXTH SUNDAY OF EASTER (Mother's Day)

Priest: Let us bring our prayers
before the Father of Jesus Christ and
our Father.

Minister: That the members of the church,
especially those who were initiated at Easter,
will receive the power of God
in living the Christian faith,
let us pray to the Lord:

That world leaders will receive the guidance
of God
in promoting peace and justice,
let us pray to the Lord:

That mothers will receive the blessing of God
in caring for their families,
let us pray to the Lord:

That those soon to graduate
will receive the goodness of God
in discovering new tasks and friends,
let us pray to the Lord:

That those who are suffering from sickness,
especially _____ and _____,
will receive the peace of God
in healing for body, mind, and spirit,
let us pray to the Lord:

That those who have died,
especially _____ and _____,
will receive the happiness of God
in living forever,
let us pray to the Lord:

+

+

Priest: We praise you, our God,
in this assembly of your people,
for your Holy Spirit
unites us to you and to your risen Son.
Answer the prayers we offer you this day,
for we make them in the name of Jesus Christ,
who is Lord for ever and ever. Amen.

May 17, 2007

ASCENSION OF THE LORD
(celebrated in some places on Sunday, May 20)

Priest: On this day when Jesus was lifted up from our midst,
let us stand before our God in solemn prayer.

Minister: That the Lord will grant wisdom and insight
to those who lead God's holy church,
let us pray to the Lord:

That the Lord will share the wealth
of the glorious heritage in Christ with
all nations,
let us pray to the Lord:

That the Lord will enlighten the minds
of those
who face the future with apprehension
and uncertainty,
let us pray to the Lord:

That the Lord will empower the oppressed of
the earth
with the strength of Christ's triumph over evil,
let us pray to the Lord:

That the Lord will raise up those who
have died,
especially _____ and _____,
and grant them everlasting joy,
let us pray to the Lord:

+

+

Priest: **Most holy God,
we ask you to answer our prayers,
so that in the time between Jesus' ascension
and his return in majesty,
we may find courage in the power of
    his blessing
and bear witness to your great love for us.
We ask this in the name of him
who has ascended to your right hand,
there to celebrate life with you and the
    Holy Spirit,
one God, for ever and ever. Amen.**

May 20, 2007

SEVENTH SUNDAY OF EASTER
(where the Ascension is celebrated on Thursday, May 17)

Priest: Let us ask God to hear these petitions,
so that the life-giving water of saving grace
may be ours in abundance.

Minister: For those who lead the church,
that they proclaim God's merciful love
in their service of all,
let us pray to the Lord:

For those who govern nations and peoples,
that they reflect God's universal love
in words and works of justice,
let us pray to the Lord:

For those who suffer from poverty
and disease,
that they know God's bountiful love
in our care and compassion,
let us pray to the Lord:

For us who worship here,
that we welcome God's abundant love in
oneness of heart,
let us pray to the Lord:

For those who have died,
especially _____ and _____,
that they receive God's everlasting love
in the glory of heaven,
let us pray to the Lord:

✢

✢

Priest: **Lord Most High,
as Jesus, your Son, prayed for us,
so we pray for one another.
Let your love sustain us
this day and every day,
so that we will be one with you and your
    beloved Son,
and rejoice in you for ever and ever. Amen.**

May 27, 2007

PENTECOST

Priest: The Spirit of the Lord fills the whole world,
is all-embracing, and knows the thoughts of
 our hearts.
In the power of the Spirit who helps us to
 pray rightly,
let us ask God to renew us and the face of
 the earth.

Minister: That the church will proclaim God's love
 with boldness,
let us pray to the Lord:

That nations will accept God's call to live in
 holiness and peace,
let us pray to the Lord:

That graduates will use God's gifts for the
 common good,
let us pray to the Lord:

That farmers will receive God's strength in
 seedtime and harvest,
let us pray to the Lord:

That the poor and the suffering
will rejoice in God's deliverance
 and refreshment,
let us pray to the Lord:

That those who have died,
especially _____ and _____,
will for ever celebrate God's marvels
    accomplished in them,
let us pray to the Lord:

+

+

Priest: **Father of light,
from whom every good gift comes,
send your Spirit into our lives with the power
    of a mighty wind.
Enlighten our minds by the flame of
    your wisdom;
open our hands to do your work well;
open our mouths to sing your praise,
through Jesus Christ, our Lord. Amen.**

May 28, 2007

MEMORIAL DAY (United States of America)

Priest: **Confident that all who have died in Christ will be raised to life with him for ever, let us offer these petitions to our compassionate God.**

Minister: **For the mercy of God upon our brothers and sisters, especially those who gave their lives in defending our country, and for their everlasting happiness with all the saints, let us pray to the Lord:**

For the renewal of baptismal grace in all the members of the church, let us pray to the Lord:

For safe travel and enjoyable leisure this holiday weekend and throughout the summer months, let us pray to the Lord:

For the power of Christ's holy cross and glorious resurrection that saves us in our need, let us pray to the Lord:

For the final destruction of sin, death, and the grave by the triumph of the risen Christ, let us pray to the Lord:

+

+

Priest: Holy, immortal God,
give to all who served you in this life
a place of everlasting refreshment, light
    and peace.
Grant that we,
in company with all those who have fallen
    asleep in Christ,
may praise and thank you for ever and ever.
    Amen.

June 3, 2007

HOLY TRINITY

Priest: God's Holy Spirit now leads us into prayer
and gives us the assurance that God will hear
    our petitions.

Minister: For the Christian churches,
that they be one in the unifying love of the
    Father, Son and Holy Spirit,
let us pray to the Lord:

For civil authorities,
that they intensify their efforts
to establish peace and justice throughout
    the world,
let us pray to the Lord:

For the homeless and the hungry, the sick and
    the dying,
that they receive consolation from the God
    who saves,
let us pray to the Lord:

For all who have gathered here,
that we welcome the love of God,
poured into our hearts in this Eucharist,
let us pray to the Lord:

For those who have died,
especially _____ and _____,
that they share the glory of the Triune God,
let us pray to the Lord:

+

+

Priest: Lord God, have mercy on us and answer
  our prayers.
Let the love which unites the Persons of
  the Trinity
shape our lives and the lives of all people.
We ask this in the name of Jesus, your Son,
who celebrates life with you and the
  Holy Spirit,
one God, for ever and ever. Amen.

June 10, 2007

BODY AND BLOOD OF CHRIST

Priest: Let us ask our generous God to be mindful of us in our need.

Minister: That those who lead the churches
will help us live as the one Body of Christ,
let us pray to the Lord:

That national and local agencies
will satisfy the human hunger for peace
    and justice,
let us pray to the Lord:

That those who suffer in body, mind, and spirit
will be gladdened by many signs
of divine and human love for them,
let us pray to the Lord:

That this assembly
will delight in Christ's gift of himself in
    the Eucharist,
let us pray to the Lord:

That the dead,
especially _____ and _____,
will be raised up to sing God's praise
    in heaven,
let us pray to the Lord:

✢

✢

Priest: **God our Father,
nothing is lacking to those who love you.
Multiply your blessings among us
for our good and your glory.
Yours be the praise and the glory
through Jesus Christ, for ever and ever. Amen.**

June 15, 2007

SACRED HEART

Priest: As we honor the Most Sacred Heart of Jesus,
formed by the Holy Spirit in the womb of the Virgin Mother,
let us present our needs to almighty God.

Minister: That Jesus, fountain of life and holiness,
will keep the church holy and pure
in its witness to the Gospel,
let us pray to the Lord:

That Jesus, ruler and center of all hearts,
will lead the nations in the ways of peace,
let us pray to the Lord:

That Jesus, source of all consolation,
will give comfort to the sick and the dying,
especially _____ and _____,
let us pray to the Lord:

That Jesus, salvation of those who trust in him,
will draw us to himself
in his saving death and resurrection,
let us pray to the Lord:

That Jesus, hope of those who die in him,
will raise up all the faithful departed,
especially _____ and _____,
let us pray to the Lord:

+

+

Priest: **God of mercy,**
your beloved Son accepted death on a cross
  for us.
Receive our prayers for the sake of him
whose heart was filled with your infinite love.
We ask this through our Good Shepherd,
  Jesus Christ,
who is Lord for ever and ever. Amen.

June 17, 2007

ELEVENTH SUNDAY IN ORDINARY TIME
(Father's Day)

Priest: Jesus Christ loved us and gave himself up for us,
so that we might be put right with God.
Let us pray for our needs and the needs of people everywhere.

Minister: That the leaders of the church will live for God
by seeking the unity of all Christians,
let us pray to the Lord:

That the nations and peoples of the earth
will live for God
by embracing justice and peace,
let us pray to the Lord:

That fathers will live for God
by generously serving their families in love,
let us pray to the Lord:

That those oppressed by any need
will live for God
by believing firmly in Jesus Christ,
let us pray to the Lord:

That we who worship here will live for God
by forgiving each other from our hearts,
let us pray to the Lord:

That all who have died,
especially _____ and _____,
will live for God
by sharing in Christ's resurrection,
let us pray to the Lord:

+

+

Priest: Lord, though we are sinners,
you have taken away our guilt.
Shelter us and all people in answer to
    our prayers,
so that we may rejoice in you,
both now and for ever. Amen.

June 24, 2007

NATIVITY OF ST. JOHN THE BAPTIST

Priest: In company with the great Mother of God,
 Mary most-holy,
with John the Forerunner, and with all
 the saints,
let us commend ourselves and the whole
 world to the mercy of God
in these petitions.

Minister: That, with the courage of John,
Christians dare to proclaim God's Word to
 those in need,
let us pray to the Lord:

That, with the self-sacrifice of John,
we give ourselves to generous service of others,
let us pray to the Lord:

That, with the faith of John,
that we trust in the saving power of
 Jesus Christ,
let us pray to the Lord:

That, with the humility of John,
we find strength for our weakness
in God's surpassing greatness,
let us pray to the Lord:

That, sharing eternal life with John and all
 the saints,
those who have died,
especially _____ and _____,
rejoice in God's salvation for ever,
let us pray to the Lord:

✢

✢

Priest: God of holiness,
your hand rested on John the Baptist
and made him a mighty herald for your Son.
As we celebrate John's birth,
help us by his example and intercession
to serve you with heartfelt love.
We ask this through Christ our Lord. Amen.

June 29, 2007

SS. PETER AND PAUL, APOSTLES

Priest: In company with Saints Peter and Paul,
who prayed for all the churches of God,
let us confidently call upon their Father
and ours.

Minister: That Pope _____, the successor of
Peter, and all pastors
will strengthen us in the apostolic faith,
let us pray to the Lord:

That leaders of nations
will protect the church from persecution
and harassment,
let us pray to the Lord:

That those who are suffering
for who they are or for what they believe
will find strength in the Lord
who is at their side,
let us pray to the Lord:

That apostles, prophets, and teachers
will build up this community as the Body
of Christ,
let us pray to the Lord:

That those who have kept the faith in death,
especially _____ and _____,
will rejoice with Peter and Paul around God's
throne for ever,
let us pray to the Lord:

✢

✢

Priest: **God of saints and sinners,
by the power of the Holy Spirit
Peter and Paul bore courageous witness
to the death and resurrection of your Son.
Hear our prayer for your blessings,
that we may be more faithful witnesses
to the truth of the Gospel,
the good news of Jesus Christ,
both now and for ever. Amen.**

July 1, 2007

THIRTEENTH SUNDAY IN ORDINARY TIME
(Canada Day)

Priest: Having heard the words of everlasting life,
let us bring our needs to God in this
common prayer.

Minister: For the ministers of the church,
that they experience the joy of
generous service
for the reign of God,
let us pray to the Lord:

For public officials,
that they achieve success in their efforts
to build up the human family,
let us pray to the Lord:

For the people of Canada on this, their
national day,
that they know the blessings of prosperity,
harmony, and justice,
let us pray to the Lord:

For all who travel and vacation during
this season,
that they enjoy safety and refreshment in their
leisure time,
let us pray to the Lord:

For us who celebrate the Eucharist in
this place,
that we find renewed strength in following
the Lord Jesus,
let us pray to the Lord:

For those who have died,
especially _____ and _____,
that they know delight at God's right hand
    for ever,
let us pray to the Lord:

✢

✢

Priest: Lord God, you have set us on the way
    of discipleship.
As we journey together,
we ask you to answer our prayers.
Grant that your Son be for us and for
    all people
our joyful inheritance,
this day and every day, both now and for ever.
    Amen.

July 4, 2007

INDEPENDENCE DAY (United States of America)

Priest: On this holiday,
we remember that the justice of God is like rock,
God's mercy like pure flowing water.
Let us ask God to take away our sinfulness
as we celebrate God's goodness,
so that we may ask God's gifts for our country
with thankful hearts.

(Select from the following intentions as desired.)

Minister: For a clear message of God's love and power
in the church's ministry of the Gospel,
let us pray to the Lord:

For insight and courage
in federal, state, and local government,
let us pray to the Lord:

For justice and humility, fairness
    and compassion,
in the administration of law
and in the defense of our people,
let us pray to the Lord:

For mutual care and cooperation
and a concern for the good of all
in industry, commerce and agriculture,
let us pray to the Lord:

For wholesomeness and integrity
in art and music, theatre and entertainment,
in sport and leisure,
let us pray to the Lord:

For a vision of social good
and for service to the truth
in every mode of communication,
in journalism and literature,
radio, television, and the Internet,
let us pray to the Lord:

For a deepening of knowledge in the mind
as well as a maturing of the spirit
in family and school and college,
let us pray to the Lord:

For a community that cares in word and deed
in the service of those in need and sickness,
in anxiety and suffering,
let us pray to the Lord:

For everlasting life for those who have died,
especially _____ and _____,
and for all who gave their lives for
    our freedom,
let us pray to the Lord:

+

+

Priest: Great and eternal God,
you have made all the peoples of the earth for
    your glory,
to serve you in freedom and peace.
Give to the people of our country
what they ask of you this day,
so that they may live humbly before you,
devoted to all that is true and good and just.
We make this prayer through Christ our Lord.
    Amen.

July 8, 2007

FOURTEENTH SUNDAY IN ORDINARY TIME

Priest: Let us ask peace and mercy for all in need,
both in this community and throughout all
the earth.

Minister: That Christians will know the Lord's power
in living as a new creation,
let us pray to the Lord:

That nations and peoples will know the
Lord's power
in all that leads to peace and justice,
let us pray to the Lord:

That the poor and the oppressed
will know the Lord's power
in their deliverance from suffering,
let us pray to the Lord:

That we who follow the rule of life in
Christ Jesus
will know the Lord's power in this Eucharist,
let us pray to the Lord:

That those who have died,
especially _____ and _____,
will know the Lord's power in fullness of joy,
let us pray to the Lord:

✢

✢

Priest: **Comforting God,
refuse not our prayers,
so that our hearts may rejoice
in your mighty works.
We ask this through Christ our Lord. Amen.**

July 15, 2007

FIFTEENTH SUNDAY IN ORDINARY TIME

Priest: Let us turn to the Lord with fervent prayer,
asking that the Lord's voice will renew in us
our love for God and neighbor.

Minister: For the leaders of the churches,
that they will heed the Lord's voice
calling Christians to unity,
let us pray to the Lord:

For those who seek solutions to global
  economic problems,
that they will obey the Lord's voice
calling them to promote justice and peace,
let us pray to the Lord:

For those who suffer from illness
  and violence,
that they will hear the Lord's voice
calling them to wholeness,
let us pray to the Lord:

For us who celebrate the Eucharist this day,
that we will respond to the Lord's voice
calling us to mutual love,
let us pray to the Lord:

For those who have died,
especially _____ and _____,
that they will rejoice in the Lord's voice
calling them to everlasting life,
let us pray to the Lord:

✛

✛

Priest: Gracious and merciful God,
you have given us the fullness of your love in
 Christ Jesus.
May the words of our mouths,
the thoughts of our hearts,
and the work of our hands,
proclaim the holiness we find in your
 beloved Son.
Help us live as members of his Body,
one with you and with each other
in the bond of love,
both now and for ever. Amen.

July 22, 2007

SIXTEENTH SUNDAY IN ORDINARY TIME

Priest: Let us bring our needs to the God of glory,
who has come close to us in Jesus Christ.

Minister: That all who serve the community of believers
will live in the Lord's presence
through their ministry,
let us pray to the Lord:

That nations and peoples will live in the
 Lord's presence
through their commitment to peace,
let us pray to the Lord:

That those who suffer from neglect and abuse
will live in the Lord's presence
through our words and deeds of compassion,
let us pray to the Lord:

That we will live in the Lord's presence
through God's gifts to us in this Eucharist,
let us pray to the Lord:

That those who have died,
especially _____ and _____,
will live in the Lord's presence
through sharing Christ's resurrection,
let us pray to the Lord:

✛

✛

Priest: **Lord, with Mary of Bethany
we open wide our ears to hear your word;
with Martha, we open wide our hands to do
  your work.
Let our prayers today
center our lives on your Son, Jesus Christ,
who is Lord for ever and ever. Amen.**

July 29, 2007

SEVENTEENTH SUNDAY IN ORDINARY TIME

Priest: Let us call upon God our Savior in fervent prayer.

Minister: That the all-powerful God
will be the church's power for good,
let us pray to the Lord:

That the all-reconciling God
will be the reconciliation of states
and peoples,
let us pray to the Lord:

That the all-saving God
will be the salvation of the sick and the poor,
the hungry and the homeless,
let us pray to the Lord:

That the all-protecting God
will be the protection of all who defend us,
especially police officers and firefighters,
let us pray to the Lord:

That the all-strong God
will be the strength of this parish community,
let us pray to the Lord:

That the all-merciful God
will be the mercy of those who have died,
especially _____ and _____,
let us pray to the Lord:

+

+

Priest: **Generous God,
as Jesus taught us, we knock on the door of
 your mercy,
and seek your good gifts for body, soul,
 and spirit.
Give us what you have inspired us
to ask of you in faith,
through Jesus Christ, our Lord. Amen.**

August 5, 2007

EIGHTEENTH SUNDAY IN ORDINARY TIME

Priest: With great confidence,
let us ask the Lord's kindness and faithfulness
for us and for all God's servants.

Minister: For the welfare of the holy church of God
and for the well-being of the human family,
let us pray to the Lord:

For the elimination of disease, famine,
and war,
and for an end to hatred and violence,
especially in the Middle East and in Africa,
let us pray to the Lord:

For the recovery of the sick
and for the deliverance of the oppressed,
let us pray to the Lord:

For seasonable weather, sufficient rainfall, and
bountiful harvests,
and for a just return for human labor,
let us pray to the Lord:

For the consolation of the dying
and for the eternal happiness of those who
have died,
especially _____ and _____,
let us pray to the Lord:

✢

✢

Priest: **Father,
we rejoice in your never-failing help.
Show us the greatness of your love,
and answer our prayers in your great mercy.
We ask this through Christ our Lord. Amen.**

August 12, 2007

NINETEENTH SUNDAY IN ORDINARY TIME

Priest: As the people the Lord has blessed in
    Christ Jesus,
let us ask God's blessing on us and on
    our world
in these prayers.

Minister: That the Lord's kindness
will be upon the members of the church
and be their source of faith,
let us pray to the Lord:

That the Lord's kindness
will be upon all peoples of the earth
and be their deliverance from every danger,
let us pray to the Lord:

That the Lord's kindness
will be upon those weakened by mental and
    physical suffering,
especially _____ and _____,
and be their comfort in distress,
let us pray to the Lord:

That the Lord's kindness
will be upon us who worship here
and be our help in every need,
let us pray to the Lord:

That the Lord's kindness
will be upon all who have died,
especially _____ and _____,
and be their peace for ever,
let us pray to the Lord:

+

+

Priest: **Increase our faith, ever-faithful God,
so that with your holy ones of old
we may embrace your kindness in our lives
and share it with others
according to your will.
We ask this through Christ our Lord. Amen.**

August 15, 2007

ASSUMPTION OF MARY

Priest: In the assumption of Mary into heaven,
we see the glory that God calls us to share.
As we celebrate the mighty deeds
that God's love accomplished in her,
we confidently ask God to hear our prayers.

Minister: That the church, like Mary,
will rejoice to share Christ's victory
  over death,
let us pray to the Lord:

That world leaders
will ensure that their countries' might
  and wealth
are used for peace and not for war,
let us pray to the Lord:

That those who lift up the spirits
of the poor, the homeless, and the oppressed
will never lose hope in the saving power
  of God,
let us pray to the Lord:

That we who celebrate this Eucharist
will imitate Mary's example of trust and love,
let us pray to the Lord:

That those who have died,
especially _____ and _____,
will find everlasting joy in God their Savior,
let us pray to the Lord:

Let us remember our own intentions.

[pause for silent prayer]

For these, let us pray to the Lord:

+

+

Priest: Mary's God and our God,
you have blessed us with the gift of your
    beloved Son
and his most-holy mother.
Look with favor upon our prayers
for your continued blessings.
Grant that we, like Mary,
proclaim your greatness in all that you
    accomplish for us.
We ask this through Christ our Lord. Amen.

August 19, 2007

TWENTIETH SUNDAY IN ORDINARY TIME

Priest: Faith is God's gift to those who doubt,
courage to those who are afraid,
and strength to those who are weak.
Let us ask God to hear these petitions.

Minister: That the church will receive the power
  of Jesus
in its witness to his Gospel,
let us pray to the Lord:

That public officials will receive the strength
  of Jesus
in their defense of human rights,
let us pray to the Lord:

That the young and the aged, the poor and
  the suffering,
will receive the consolation of Jesus in
  their need,
let us pray to the Lord:

That we who celebrate this Eucharist
will receive the perseverance of Jesus
in our life of faith,
let us pray to the Lord:

That those who kept their eyes fixed on Jesus
  in this life,
especially _____ and _____,
will receive the vision of Jesus in heaven,
let us pray to the Lord:

\+

\+

Priest: **Father,
trusting in your goodness
we ask you to answer our prayers.
Come to our aid, come to our aid,
so that the living flame of love
in the heart of Jesus and in our hearts
will brighten our world.
We ask this through Christ our Lord. Amen.**

August 26, 2007

TWENTY-FIRST SUNDAY IN ORDINARY TIME

Priest: With trust in God as wide as our need,
let us offer these petitions.

Minister: For the community of believers in this and
every place,
and for those who witness to God's love for
all peoples,
let us pray to the Lord:

For the children of God throughout the earth,
especially those forced to live less than the
life for which God made them,
let us pray to the Lord:

For the poor and the ill,
in our midst and far away,
and for those who care for their needs
in humility,
let us pray to the Lord:

For us who know the kindness and fidelity of
the Lord in our worship,
and for those who have strayed from
Christ's church,
let us pray to the Lord:

For those who have been called
to God's kingdom in death,
especially _____ and _____,
and for those who mourn them,
let us pray to the Lord:

✢

✢

Priest: God of holiness, as you receive our prayers,
welcome us to your table with all your
holy ones.
Let us share your feast of life and love,
both now and for ever. Amen.

September 2, 2007

TWENTY-SECOND SUNDAY IN ORDINARY TIME

Priest: How great is the mercy of the Lord!
God's loving-kindness is everlasting!
Let us pray for the church, the world,
and for people everywhere.

Minister: That God's goodness will provide
more vocations
for the church's mission,
let us pray to the Lord:

That God's goodness will provide
abundant help
for all who suffer in body or spirit,
especially _____ and _____,
let us pray to the Lord:

That God's goodness will provide sure hope
for those who have lost their way,
let us pray to the Lord:

That God's goodness will provide
generous gifts
for this assembly of worshipers,
let us pray to the Lord:

That God's goodness will provide an
everlasting home
for all who have died,
especially _____ and _____,
let us pray to the Lord:

✢

✢

Priest: **Gracious God,
let your infinite goodness be ours
in answer to these prayers,
for we make them in the name of your
 beloved Son,
Jesus Christ, who is Lord for ever and ever.
 Amen.**

September 3, 2007

LABOR DAY (United States of America and Canada)

Priest: God works for our good, now and always.
On this Labor Day,
let us pray for our needs
and those of people everywhere.

Minister: For the peace and unity
of the holy church of God throughout
    the world,
let us pray to the Lord:

For the well-being of the human family,
and for peace among all nations,
let us pray to the Lord:

For a just return for human labor
and for a safe environment for all workers,
let us pray to the Lord:

For the elimination of slavery
    and exploitation,
and for an end to poverty, sickness,
    and unemployment,
let us pray to the Lord:

For the building of a more humane world,
and for deliverance from pain, fear,
    and distress,
let us pray to the Lord:

For the everlasting joy
of those who have entered God's eternal rest,
especially _____ and _____,
and for the comforting of those who
    mourn them,
let us pray to the Lord:

+

+

Priest: God of work and rest,
we join our petitions to the powerful prayers
of Saint Joseph the Worker.
Grant us what we need, this day and
    every day,
through Jesus Christ, our Lord. Amen.

September 9, 2007

TWENTY-THIRD SUNDAY IN ORDINARY TIME

Priest: Let us call upon the Lord, our refuge in every age,
and offer fervent prayer for all in need.

Minister: That the Lord's gracious care
will sustain the church in its witness to the Gospel,
let us pray to the Lord:

That the Lord's gracious care
will protect the rulers of nations and their people,
let us pray to the Lord:

That the Lord's gracious care
will deliver the poor and the oppressed from suffering,
let us pray to the Lord:

That the Lord's gracious care
will help us to know God's will and to do it,
let us pray to the Lord:

That the Lord's gracious care
will become everlasting life and joy
for those who have died,
especially _____ and _____,
let us pray to the Lord:

+

+

Priest: **Lord,
your Holy Spirit guides us on the path
    of discipleship.
By our prayers,
renew the power of that Spirit in every heart,
so that we may judge wisely the things
    of earth
and love the things of heaven.
We ask this through Christ our Lord. Amen.**

September 16, 2007

TWENTY-FOURTH SUNDAY IN ORDINARY TIME
(Catechetical Sunday)

Priest: **My sisters and brothers,
let us pray that the grace of Jesus Christ
will be abundant for us and for all people
in need.**

Minister: **For those who teach the Christian faith
in our parish, in our diocese and throughout
the world,
let us pray to the Lord:**

**For those who promote justice and peace in
this and every land,
let us pray to the Lord:**

**For those who suffer from poverty
and sickness,
especially _____ and _____,
let us pray to the Lord:**

**For us who proclaim the Lord's praise in
this Eucharist,
let us pray to the Lord:**

**For those who have died in the hope of
everlasting life,
especially _____ and _____,
let us pray to the Lord:**

+

+

Priest: **Great is your compassion, O Lord,
toward us and all your people.
Let your goodness be seen in answer to
 our prayers.
Honor and glory be yours in Christ Jesus,
both now and for ever. Amen.**

September 23, 2007

TWENTY-FIFTH SUNDAY IN ORDINARY TIME

Priest: The Lord Jesus presents our needs to God
and protects those who dwell in him.
Let us ask him to unite us in his peace
as we pray in his name.

Minister: That leaders of the church
will receive the Lord's guidance in
their ministry,
let us pray to the Lord:

That leaders of governments and those
in authority
will imitate the Lord's love for justice
in their words and deeds,
let us pray to the Lord:

That victims of domestic and gang violence
will enjoy the Lord's healing in their need,
let us pray to the Lord:

That we who worship here
will live in the power of the Lord's truth,
let us pray to the Lord:

That those who have died,
especially _____ and _____,
will rejoice in the Lord's salvation in heaven,
let us pray to the Lord:

Let us remember our particular needs.

[pause for silent prayer]

For these needs, let us pray to the Lord:

+

+

Priest: **Lord God, maker of heaven and earth,
we raise our hands and hearts to you in
 fervent prayer.
In your love, guard us from every danger
and grant us your salvation.
We ask this through Christ our Lord. Amen.**

September 30, 2007

TWENTY-SIXTH SUNDAY IN ORDINARY TIME

Priest: With confidence in God's love and mercy,
let us present our needs to the Lord.

Minister: For Pope _____, (Arch) Bishop
_____,
and all who serve the church,
that God's strength be theirs
as they witness to Jesus Christ,
let us pray to the Lord:

For leaders of governments,
that God's protection be theirs
as they work for justice and peace,
let us pray to the Lord:

For the poor, the hungry and the homeless,
the sick and the injured,
that God's deliverance be theirs
as they receive our words of hope and deeds
    of love,
let us pray to the Lord:

For those who have died,
especially _____ and _____,
that God's joy be theirs
as they celebrate eternal life,
let us pray to the Lord:

Let us remember our particular intentions.

[pause for silent prayer]

**That God's help be ours in every need,
let us pray to the Lord:**

+

+

Priest: **God of all consolation,
hear our prayers for your good gifts.
Help us to live as unselfishly
as did your Son, Jesus Christ,
and so come to live with him in your presence,
for ever and ever. Amen.**

October 7, 2007

TWENTY-SEVENTH SUNDAY IN ORDINARY TIME (Respect Life Sunday)

Priest: With faith in Christ Jesus, who gives us life in abundance,
let us pray for the needs of all God's children.

Minister: For the church's proclamation and promotion of every effort to establish God's peace throughout the world,
let us pray to the Lord:

For an opening of every heart to those who lack the necessities of human life,
let us pray to the Lord:

For wisdom to recognize and reverence every person as God's gift, especially the unborn, the elderly, the terminally ill and the desperately poor,
let us pray to the Lord:

For the strengthening of all who are afflicted in body, mind, and spirit,
let us pray to the Lord:

For fullness of life in God's presence for all who have died,
especially _____ and _____,
let us pray to the Lord:

✢

✢

Priest: **Gracious God, source of all life,
you have called us by name
and made us your people.
We ask a full portion of your goodness
in every human heart.
Let our faith and love establish our lives
   in peace,
for the life of the world.
We ask this through Christ our Lord. Amen.**

October 14, 2007

TWENTY-EIGHTH SUNDAY IN ORDINARY TIME

Priest: Let us pray for all in need,
here in our midst and throughout all the earth.

Minister: That Christians will know the Lord's
saving power
in the Word of God and the sacraments,
let us pray to the Lord:

That nations and peoples will know the Lord's
saving power
in all that leads to justice and peace,
let us pray to the Lord:

That the sick and the poor will know the
Lord's saving power
in their deliverance from suffering,
let us pray to the Lord:

That we who seek to live with Christ
will know the Lord's saving power in
this Eucharist,
let us pray to the Lord:

That those who have died,
especially _____ and _____,
will know the Lord's saving power
in reigning with Christ,
let us pray to the Lord:

Let us ask the Lord's saving power as we remember our particular needs.

[pause for silent prayer]

For all our needs, let us pray to the Lord:

+

+

Priest: **Lord our God,
how tremendous are your deeds, how marvelous your works!
Answer our prayers,
for with the grateful leper in the Gospel,
we trust in your Son's power
to help and save us.
With Naaman we say:
Yours be the praise and the glory, for ever and ever! Amen.**

October 21, 2007

TWENTY-NINTH SUNDAY IN ORDINARY TIME
(World Mission Sunday)

Priest: Our help in every need is from the Lord.
In company with Christ, let us offer
   these petitions
to the God who upholds our lives.

Minister: That missionaries at home and abroad
will receive the Lord's protection
as they preach the Word of God,
let us pray to the Lord:

That leaders of governments
will imitate the Lord's love for justice
in their words and deeds,
let us pray to the Lord:

That the sick, especially _____ and
_____,
will enjoy the Lord's healing and comfort,
let us pray to the Lord:

That we will welcome the Lord's
   saving wisdom
in the Scriptures that enliven our prayer
   and work,
let us pray to the Lord:

That those who have died,
especially _____ and _____,
will rejoice in the Lord's salvation for ever,
let us pray to the Lord:

┼

┼

Priest: God our strength, we turn to you.
Show us your great love
in answer to these prayers,
and hear those who call out to you
day and night, in every place.
We ask this through Christ our Lord. Amen.

October 28, 2007

THIRTIETH SUNDAY IN ORDINARY TIME
(Reformation Sunday)

Priest: Let us call upon the Lord,
who is always close to those who seek mercy.

Minister: For the holy church of God,
that it will have unity and peace throughout
   the world,
let us pray to the Lord:

For our Lutheran sisters and brothers,
that their celebration of Reformation Sunday
will deepen their love for Jesus Christ
in his Word and in his Supper,
let us pray to the Lord:

For civil authorities,
that God will direct their hearts and minds for
   our well-being,
let us pray to the Lord:

For the sick, the hungry, and the homeless,
that God working through us
will speedily answer their cries for help.
let us pray to the Lord:

For this assembly of God's people,
that we will grow in the humility of
   Jesus Christ,
let us pray to the Lord:

For all who have died,
especially _____ and _____,
that they will celebrate Christ's victory over
    sin and death
in his heavenly kingdom,
let us pray to the Lord:

Let us remember our particular needs.

[pause for silent prayer]

For these needs, let us pray to the Lord:

+

+

Priest: Lord our God,
your mercy toward the humble
    is measureless,
and your love is beyond words to describe.
Look upon us in your great kindness,
and grant us the riches of your favor,
through Jesus Christ, our Lord. Amen.

November 1, 2007

ALL SAINTS

Priest: Almighty God, out of love for us,
has made us God's children,
and has granted us communion with the
    saints in light.
Let us make our petitions with confidence,
for God will give us everything we need
to live as a holy people.

Minister: That the Lord will bless
those who are lowly and poor in spirit,
and be their inheritance for ever,
let us pray to the Lord:

That the Lord will bless
those who are in sorrow,
and be their consolation for ever,
let us pray to the Lord:

That the Lord will bless
those who hunger and thirst for eternal life,
and be their feast for ever,
let us pray to the Lord:

That the Lord will bless
those who search for God with a sincere heart,
and be their vision for ever,
let us pray to the Lord:

That the Lord will bless
those who suffer persecution for
    holiness' sake,
and be their refuge for ever,
let us pray to the Lord:

That the Lord will bless
those who have died believing in
    Jesus' resurrection,
especially _____ and _____,
and be their joy for ever,
let us pray to the Lord:

+

+

Priest: **Ever-living God,
we are gathered as your family
to praise your name and honor your holy ones.
In your kindness, answer our prayers
and the prayers the saints offer on our behalf.
Let us share their communion of life and love,
for ever and ever. Amen.**

November 2, 2007

COMMEMORATION OF ALL THE FAITHFUL DEPARTED (ALL SOULS)

Priest: Blessed is the Lord our God,
ruler of life and death,
for raising the beloved Son as the first-born
  from the dead.
In his life-giving name,
let us pray that all who sleep in Christ
will awake to share his glory.

Minister: The Lord Jesus raised the widow's son to life.
In his name, let us ask God's unending life
for our deceased relatives and friends.
For this, let us pray to the Lord:

The Lord Jesus wept at the death of Lazarus.
In his name, let us ask God's consolation
for all who mourn.
For this, let us pray to the Lord:

The Lord Jesus promised paradise to the
  repentant thief.
In his name, let us ask God's happiness
for all who died in great misery and suffering.
For this, let us pray to the Lord:

The Lord Jesus fed the hungry and healed
  the sick.
In his name, let us ask God's refreshment
for victims of neglect, starvation and disease.
For this, let us pray to the Lord:

The Lord Jesus redeemed his faithful ones
through the cross.
In his name, let us ask God's salvation
for our fellow-parishioners,
especially _____ and _____,
and for all God's servants.
For this, let us pray to the Lord:

+

+

Priest: Holy, immortal God,
you are the source of everlasting life
for all your people.
Grant forgiveness and peace
to those whom we remember today at
    your altar.
We ask this in the name of Jesus the Lord.
    Amen.

November 4, 2007

THIRTY-FIRST SUNDAY IN ORDINARY TIME

Priest: Because Jesus delights in seeking us and
saving us,
let us confidently present our needs to the
God of mercy in his name.

Minister: For our Holy Father, our bishop, our pastor,
and the staff of this parish,
let us pray to the Lord:

For the members of this community of faith,
and for those preparing to become members,
let us pray to the Lord:

For our national, state, and local officials,
let us pray to the Lord:

For the unemployed, the hungry, and
the homeless,
and for those who are ill or injured,
especially _____ and _____,
let us pray to the Lord:

For those who are lost
in the darkness of addiction to alcohol, drugs,
and gambling,
let us pray to the Lord:

For the faithful departed,
especially _____ and _____,
let us pray to the Lord:

✢

✢

Priest: **Lord God,**
our need for your mercy is great,
but your love for us and for all people is
far greater.
Hear and answer the prayers we present to
you this day,
for we make them in the name of your
beloved Son, Jesus Christ,
who is Lord for ever and ever. Amen.

November 11, 2007

THIRTY-SECOND SUNDAY IN ORDINARY TIME

Priest: Let us call upon the Lord,
who is near to us both in life and in death.

Minister: That the Lord's strength
will empower all believers
for every good deed and word,
let us pray to the Lord:

That the Lord's guidance
will direct our public servants
along the paths of justice and peace,
let us pray to the Lord:

That the Lord's protection
will shield all military personnel from danger,
let us pray to the Lord:

That the Lord's salvation
will speedily deliver the people of this and
    every country
from poverty, hunger, and homelessness,
let us pray to the Lord:

That the Lord's consolation
will comfort the sick and the dying,
let us pray to the Lord:

That the Lord's mercy
will embrace those who have died,
especially those killed in warfare,
and also _____ and _____,
let us pray to the Lord:

✢

✢

Priest: **God our Savior,
your kindness extends to all people
and your faithfulness knows no limits.
Answer our prayers for the sake of him
whose death won our everlasting life,
your Son, Jesus Christ,
who lives and reigns for ever and ever. Amen.**

November 18, 2007

THIRTY-THIRD SUNDAY IN ORDINARY TIME

Priest: **Let us present our prayers to the Lord, who has come to rule the earth in Jesus Christ**

Minister: **That the members of the church will receive renewed strength in God's love, let us pray to the Lord:**

That all nations and peoples will find lasting peace in God's plan for this world, let us pray to the Lord:

That the ill and infirm will enjoy abundant comfort in God's healing, let us pray to the Lord:

That all who worship here will place sure confidence in God's salvation, let us pray to the Lord:

That the dying and those who have died, especially _____ and _____, will know eternal joy in God's reign, let us pray to the Lord:

✢

✢

Priest: **All-holy God,**
let your sun of righteousness, our Lord
    Jesus Christ,
rise in our hearts and brighten our days.
Draw us to him in this Eucharist,
so that we may welcome him now,
and live with him in your presence,
for ever and ever. Amen.

November 22, 2007

THANKSGIVING DAY (United States of America)

Priest: **The earth has yielded its fruit,
for God has blessed us generously.
As we remember to thank God
for the many signs of God's goodness,
let us ask God's blessing upon our world
in these prayers.**

Minister: For strength in the Lord's service,
that we may be united in thankfulness before
    our God,
let us pray to the Lord:

For the enduring love
that we glimpse in the ministry of Jesus,
that we may embrace the salvation of our God,
let us pray to the Lord:

For the gifts of the Holy Spirit,
that we may do all that pleases our God,
let us pray to the Lord:

For the healing of the sick, the feeding of
    the hungry,
and the consolation of the afflicted,
that they may know the deliverance of
    our God,
let us pray to the Lord:

For the peace of those who have died,
especially _____ and _____,
that they may celebrate the love of our God,
let us pray to the Lord:

Let us remember our particular needs.

[pause for silent prayer]

**For the well-being of our families
and of all who are gathered here,
that we may rest secure
under the protection of our God,
let us pray to the Lord:**

✢

✢

Priest: **Giver of all good gifts,
we ask you to accept our thanks
and to hear our prayers.
As you have made our land bear a
    rich harvest,
make our hearts fruitful
with the life and love of your Son,
    Jesus Christ,
who is Lord for ever and ever. Amen.**

November 25, 2007

OUR LORD JESUS CHRIST THE KING

Priest: In union with Christ our King,
let us ask God to hear and answer our prayers.

Minister: That the members of Christ's Body
will become like their Head
in his suffering and in his glory,
let us pray to the Lord:

That leaders of nations
will become like the Son of David
in his humility,
let us pray to the Lord:

That, as we commemorate World AIDS
    Awareness Day on Saturday,
those who are poured out in anguish,
especially those living with HIV and AIDS,
will become like God's Suffering Servant
in his fullness of life,
let us pray to the Lord:

That those who are captives to self-love
will become like the crucified Lord
in his love for others,
let us pray to the Lord:

That those who have died,
especially _____ and _____,
will become like their risen Savior
in his triumph over death,
let us pray to the Lord:

✝

✝

Priest: **Almighty and eternal God,
you willed to reconcile all things in your
     beloved Son,
the King and center of our hearts.
Help us to live the truth of his kingship,
so that we may share the lot of the saints
     in light.
Accompany us on the way to your house,
and, at journey's end,
give us everlasting joy in your kingdom.
We ask this through Christ our Lord. Amen.**